Little Thoughts from Great Cats

Margaret Peat

Little Thoughts from Great Cats

ɪ̖ρ
Editing, design and layout by Life Publications
www.lifepublications.org.uk

Dedication

This book is dedicated to Suzanne
who taught me to love cats....

Little Thoughts from Great Cats

Commendations

People often say cats have nine lives. As you turn these pages, there's a lot these animals can show us about living the life we have.

Written with warmth and humour *Little Thoughts From Great Cats* is an uplifting and thought provoking read. Margaret's understanding of cats and their endearing but sometimes unfathomable traits shines through. They each have a tail/tale that will touch your heart...

Linda Spencer
(Long suffering owner of Sukie)

Margaret and I have been friends for many, many years and one of our great bonds is our shared love of pets – we are both devoted dog and cat lovers. If I have a concern about my current pet, I can always share it with her, confident that she understands my worries and will pray about the situation.

I have really enjoyed all these "cat stories" and can relate to so much of the quirks she captures about cat behaviour – mostly unpredictable! I have also learned a few new fascinating facts about these amazing creatures!

I love the appropriate Bible quotes and thought-provoking sections following each story. A "must read" for all cat-lovers – and hopefully potential cat-lovers!

Mary Mills
(Very compassionate owner of Mickey)

Margaret Peat is a great observer of life and sees details that others might overlook. Her attention to detail and her story telling ability is amazing. As an animal lover the cats mentioned in this book have captured Margaret's heart and her love for animals is evident in every chapter. The words of wisdom at the end of each chapter are a chance for the reader to be still and reflect on their particular life situations. The practical advice and encouragement that Margaret mentions is invaluable, and may be life changing.

Marilyn Glass
(Personally selected owner of Olly and Abi)

Anyone who's ever tried having a staring contest with a cat will be familiar with that feeling that there's so much more going on in their wee heads than they're able to verbally express. It is, of course, possible that they're just really good at not blinking!

Growing up, my mum assigned different voices to each of our cats, and so we were able to ask them all for their thoughts and advice on any given issue we were facing. I'd like to think though, that Margaret's book, *Little Thoughts from Great Cats*, is the literary expression of all that feline wisdom.

These stories are enjoyable to read, and easily relatable to anyone who's ever had a cat for a family member. They are amusing, while being thought provoking and challenging.

I am confident, that even people who are highly allergic to cats, will enjoy spending 32 days in their world.

Becky Haldane
(Proud owner of Fergal)

There is, it would seem, a cat for every season of life. Brilliantly put together, this book reveals various cats' everyday experiences and then thoughtfully uses these to help us humans see the hand of God in our daily lives too.

Jamie and Christine Tonge,
(Brave owners of Papa)

Contents

Introduction

I was definitely a reluctant cat owner. Some years ago I was working extra hours at school for a while and bought a cat to keep our dog company! He was my own very first cat. Then all at once, a whole new world opened up to me as I cared for him and got to know the world behind the whiskers.

In your hand are a set of, sometimes tongue in cheek, stories about cats of all shapes and sizes, colours, ages and personalities and the special part they played in the lives of humans. If you've ever owned a cat, you will no doubt smile at some of the things I write about as you remember those animals.

The stories are not in chronological order... you will read some from my childhood, others through the years and some more recent, all mixed together and each one has played its part in teaching me some very valuable lessons.

One of our favourite holiday haunts is Lanzarote, a place that goes to great effort to ensure that the many cats in every resort are cared for and well fed. There are a generous sprinkling of Lanzarote cats included, but also cats from Shetland, Derby, Glasgow and elsewhere in the UK.

When I wrote *Great Thoughts from a Little Dog*, a daily devotional for dog lovers, I wrote it as a niche book which I expected to last for a few months and fade into obscurity.

It most definitely is my best selling book!

So here, now is *Little Thoughts from Great Cats*, again a daily devotional over one whole month encouraging us to stop and think throughout the day, about different aspects of our lives. Following each story is a personal application for you to chew on, important words from the Bible and space for you to write your own thoughts.

I hope you enjoy reading the stories and that you are blessed by God's word too as you apply it to your life.

Margaret

Chapter 1

Andrew

I met Andrew some years ago. He arrived one evening eyeing me cautiously as he sat on the patio railings. He wasn't big but he wasn't small either and he seemed to have an anxious look in his large green eyes.

He came every afternoon after that at the same time and one day he even brought another cat along too. We called that one Sooty. But Andrew was my cat on this, our first holiday in Lanzarote. He would rub himself along the railings, appearing to need a stroke but whenever I would reach out to stroke him, after two or three times he would quickly turn as though to put a stop to that. I think really, he was marking out his territory but I liked to pretend he was being friendly. With the scent glands along his tail, forehead, lips, chin and the underside of his front paws, within just a minute of being around he had secured our apartment once again as his own territory.

Sometimes he would stay for a while, sometimes even perch on the end of a sun bed. His grey glossy coat complemented well the bright colour scheme and made our patio complete. He never outstayed his welcome though and before long after eating his fill he would be gone, off on his adventures.

Some nights, I would leave his bowl full of food and sure enough it was always empty the next morning. Occasionally we could see him down by the pool taking a little drink. Ugh! Some cats, I read, could swim but it seemed Andrew wasn't one of them. It only took a quick shake of the cat biscuit box and quick as a flash he would climb three floors to join us for a snack.

A while later, when back at Glasgow, I received an email from the couple who were holidaying in the apartment next door.

"We were out in Lanzarote again last week," it read, "and who should be meowing at the door at 3am the first morning but Samson! You just can't mistake his grey coat. He usually calls late afternoon for his dinner but a change of routine, obviously!"

"Hmmmmmm," I thought.

The following summer in Lanzarote, Andrew appeared again. After a few enquiries, not only it seemed did Andrew call at nearly forty different apartments, he enjoyed a choice of nearly forty different meals and had, it seemed, nearly forty different names!

It's amazing he's not the size of an elephant!

Andrew

How many names do you answer to? Sister, brother, mum, dad, daughter, employer, neighbour, employee? No doubt you have many different titles, and each title carries a different role.

Do you really know who you are? Do you really know why you're here on earth?

We can have many roles. Not just for family and friends but for every life that we touch each day. A smile, a kind word, a helping hand, a new friend? Who can you share something with today? Why not share love, in whatever way you can today? Be God to them – with skin on!

> From high in the skies God looks around,
> he sees all Adam's brood.
> From where he sits he overlooks all us
> earth-dwellers.
> He has shaped each person in turn;
> now he watches everything we do.
>
> *Psalm 33:13-15*

Notes:

Chapter 2

Bridget's Cat

I was six years old and excited. Something wonderful had happened in our street. Bridget had got a cat! Four year old Bridget lived next door to me with her parents and sister, Isabel, and now, her cat-brother Sam.

The day came when I was allowed to go and meet Sam, a large ginger coloured feline who seemed to prefer the large shed to the house. I was grateful he was in the garden as the shed was big and dark and dusty. I sat in the sun and admired him, with his sleek glossy fur, his long whiskers and his pointed ears

Cats spend about a third of their waking day grooming themselves, (stimulating blood to flow to their skin which regulates their body temperature). Grooming also removes their human's scent and cleans them too. Sam seemed to spend most of his life doing that from what I could tell.

Bridget was my friend and we played together often and Sam was always nearby. *I'm sure he's eating too much*, I thought as I watched him lumber down the path one day. He really did seem to enjoy his food, licking his empty plate until it shone and then setting up camp by the dustbin in case some tasty morsel should come his way.

"He really must think we're very selfish," I observed to Bridget's mum as I watched her empty some waste food into the bins and then secure the lid firmly so Sam couldn't get any for himself.

I wished I had a cat, to sleep on the end of my bed, to purr at me as I stroked him and gaze up at me waiting for me to feed him.

One day, something strange happened. Sam disappeared. He was nowhere to be found. Bridget was upset and we searched all over the garden calling out his name as we looked.

It was three days before Sam was found, in a dark corner of the large shed which he loved to hide in. He was nestled down on some old rags he'd made for a bed...with six tiny kittens by his side! Everyone looked at him in astonishment! Sam had just turned into Samantha before our very eyes...

Samantha cared for her kittens beautifully and was a model mother. As the little ones grew, one by one they left the old shed and found their own forever homes all over the district of Derby. All except Oscar that was, and he was chosen to stay and become Bridget's new *cat-brother*... unless he turned out to be Olivia, of course!

People are not always what they seem to be. Many a heart has been broken when a friend/love/spouse turned out to be a lot less than they appeared.

It works in reverse too. The neighbour who never speaks can sometimes turn out to be a good friend. The bad tempered elderly lollipop man can become human after all and you discover that the worried lady on the corner still has that young girl with hopes and dreams somewhere deep inside.

There's always a reason for behaviour and many people carry hurt or disappointment or loneliness or grief and we never know. We just see the exterior, judge them and think "that's not good enough".

Who can you find today to begin to break through their hard shell by your words or your actions? Every one of us was once an innocent child. Why not work to find that child in others today?

I don't want any of you sitting around on your hands. I don't want anyone strolling off, down some path that goes nowhere. And mark that you do this with humility and discipline – not in fits and starts, but steadily, pouring yourselves out for each other in acts of love, alert at noticing differences and quick at mending fences.

Ephesians 4:1b-3

Notes:

Chapter 3

Joshua Felix

Jock 2 had been with us two months. We had picked him up from Kevin's brother whose cat had given birth six weeks before. He made the journey with us to Scotland on a hot sunny day in July and settled well into our home alongside our dog Mary.

By the age of three months he had suitably trained us to bring home the right brand of cat food by refusing to eat anything that he didn't like (although the habit of removing it from his plate onto the floor before he ate it, forever remained a mystery to me!)

Some neighbours saw our beautiful little kitten and having recently lost their own cat, asked if there were any more where Jock came from.

We were due to call into Derby the following weekend and promised to call in and pick up Jock's brother who was still available. There wasn't a choice as the other kittens had been given homes but we duly collected the remaining kitten who was now nearly four months old and travelled back to our home in Scotland and Jock 2.

Little Thoughts from Great Cats

When Jock saw his brother, even though it had been two months since they had been together, it was amazing how they knew each other instantly. How that was, I could never understand. How do two brothers who are separated months ago, know they are connected within a moment?

Joshua Felix (JF) and Jock 2 became in separable. They became the new cats on the block! They were always together, hunting mice, chasing birds, lying in the sun and rolling around the garden in mock fights. When Jock wasn't back, I would ring next door and Suzanne would say

"JF's just in, Jock won't be long," and sure enough Jock would appear within a minute of dropping his brother off.

In the mornings, I would hear meowing outside our bedroom door. I would open the front door and Jock would run out to join his brother for another day of adventures.

Nights were filled with chasing mice and catching them sometimes too. And much to my relief the prize of a dead mouse always landed on Suzanne's doormat, not mine. Either JF was a better mouse catcher or they just loved her more than me!

Siblings can sometimes be a mixed blessing! You may have a brother or sister who you dearly love or you may have ones that you would rather not visit.

Or you may have none at all.

Whatever situation we find ourselves in there are people all around us ready to be a sister, brother, mother, father, son or daughter.

And how do you find them? Of course, by being a daughter, a son, a mother or father to them. Daughters need mothers and fathers need sons.

Relationships may not be 'blood' connected but in time they can be 'love' connected and sometimes these turn out to be the very best kind.

Do you already have daughters, sons, sisters, brothers or people you look up to as a mother or father?

Who has God placed in your life? What can you become to someone today?

Here is a simple, rule-of thumb guide for behaviour: Ask yourself what you want people to do for you, then grab the initiative and do it for them.

Matthew 7:12a

Notes:

Chapter 4

The Golf Course

I gazed out of the window of our new flat which looked down onto a golf course with the city of Glasgow beyond and the Campsie Fells in the background. As I did, I was planning the lovely morning walks the dog and I could take around the golf course each day.

Before long, plans had become reality and each morning Mary and I walked our way round the edge of the disused golf course. It was a lovely time of fresh air and time spent with God, praying for friends and listening to what He would say through all I saw and heard. In the springtime He would tell me that a time of new things was round the corner and in the rain He would remind me that He would be present through every problem I may walk through.

When our kitten, Jock, came to join our family, he was safely shut in the house for the first little while but in time, once we were sure he knew where he belonged, he became an outdoor cat. He too loved the golf course and in time, along with his brother JF he would spend many hours journeying across the great expanse. I would often look out of the window and see two little dots, one ginger and one black, far away in the distance. Always on his terms though. Any chance of my cat doing exactly what I wanted was one hundred per cent not happening!

One day I had set off on my daily walk with the dog and I happened to look back and there, some way behind us was Jock the cat. I watched him follow us right round the golf course and once we were home, off he went back to his own adventures. The next morning, he did the same but came closer and by the end of the week he was walking with us.

He continued to join us on those walks for the next eight years and at the sound of the lead it was both the dog and the cat who jumped to attention each day.

Strange that his brother JF never came. Maybe that was Jock's 'me' time. Who knows?

The Golf Course

Do you have 'me' time? Or is your life so busy there is never a moment to yourself?

'Me' time helps you order your thoughts. It helps you step out of the picture of your life and see things from afar. It helps you get things into perspective. It helps you appreciate or understand those around you better. It strengthens you to go back into stressful situations. It gives you badly needed rest or relaxation. It energises you for the road ahead and it enables you to see things more clearly.

As your life is enriched by carefully chosen, regular time apart – you, in turn can enrich the lives of others in a more effective way.

Will you plan some regular 'me' time in your life?

God, my shepherd! I don't need a thing.
You have bedded me down in lush meadows,
You find me quiet pools to drink from.
True to your word,
You let me catch my breath
and send me in the right direction.

Psalm 23:1-3

Notes:

Chapter 5

Porky

As a child, we had always owned a dog. At least as long as I remember.

I had grown up with that dog in the house and when he died, it was a shock and a huge learning curve in loss. I loved dogs. To me, dogs were loving and faithful and fun. You could walk them, dress them up, run after them and play with them. They would watch out for you, welcome you home, guard you and love you unconditionally. A dog was all I wanted in a pet.

When I heard we were to have a cat, I was distraught. I'd never known a cat and didn't want a cat. Nevertheless, dad was head of the house and decreed that, as mum wanted a cat, we would be welcoming a kitten into our family.

I was out the evening he arrived. I came home from a friend's house and there he was. Standing trembling, a tiny ball of fur in the middle of the room. He looked so small and vulnerable and well... fluffy, that it was love at first sight.

"You can call him anything you want," said my dad.

"Apart from Police..." shouted my mum from the kitchen. "I am not standing in the garden in the dead of night shouting *POLICE, POLICE* for you or anyone else!"

We named him Porky (I have no idea why) and Porky became part of our family.

Careful to give him no onions, garlic, chives, green tomatoes, raw potatoes, chocolate, grapes or raisins, and also keep him away from eating the houseplants (!!) we tried our best to produce a strong healthy kitten to cat. It seems some cats are lactose intolerant and from the gas emitting from Porky's *nether regions*, we wondered if he was too, but he loved his saucer of milk each day, purring away loudly as he drank.

Amazingly he learned instantly that my bed was so much more comfy than his. Chasing his tail for hours, running from his reflection in the mirror, dancing up and down the curtains and round the room in a mad half hour, falling in a bath full of water and drinking from the tap. Attacking the vacuum cleaner, competing with the fairy at the top of the Christmas tree until it all came crashing down three days in a row and falling asleep in the most hilarious positions, little paws peddling away as he chased those mice in his dreams. He did his best to teach us to eat 'mouse' as he got older, serving on the doormat each morning, a huge variety of delicacies from which to choose. This little kitten stole our hearts. And our home.

Over his life I discovered that everyone sees the appeal of a dog (unless you don't like dogs). My dogs have shown their best to everyone. I thought that all cats were more or less identical but I learned through Porky that each has his own individual personality and nature. A cat gives his heart to his owners alone and only they can really see the true little individual behind the whiskers.

Porky

Years later when, at twenty years old, Porky closed his eyes for the last time, he had paid back what we gave for him, a thousand times over. That's what pets do. That was Porky!

I was so glad that he chose our house as his forever home.

What would life be like without surprises?

Problems that turn out to be blessings, night which turns out to be day and rain which turns out to be sunshine.

Surprises (as opposed to shocks!) lift our spirit and refresh and rejuvenate us. They teach us not to settle into complacency but to go with the flow, see which way the wind blows and with God's help set our compass and fly.

Surprises teach us flexibility and keep us fresh in mind, body and spirit. Surprises make the world a more interesting place.

Are you ready for God's surprises today?

The world's a huge stockpile
of God-wonders and God-thoughts.
Nothing and no one
comes close to you!

Psalm 40:5a

Notes:

Little Thoughts from Great Cats

Chapter 6

The Door

I had so many jobs to do that day: prepare a talk, sort my school lessons for the afternoon, make numerous phone calls, answer emails and make the house look something like normal before I left for school.

I settled in the small room which could have been a third bedroom, but really was too small. We used it as another living room, a sort of study with a put up bed for extra visitors. Our flat consisted of three bedrooms (including this one), a sitting room, kitchen and bathroom and that was it. Plenty of room for one couple, one dog and a cat.

I laid out my paperwork on the settee where I sat and began to work. I could hear the birds outside over the golf course and opened the window to allow the fresh air to fill the room. It was a bright day outside and the three of us had already done our golf course walk that morning. I could hear the dog go into the kitchen, lap water from her bowl then I guess, lie down in the sun for a nice long nap.

Earlier, when I had passed the bathroom Jock was by his huge white drinking bowl (commonly known as the toilet). He owned a perfectly good orange bowl of his own but for some reason the freshly flushed toilet tasted so much superior! But within a couple of minutes of shutting myself in the room, I knew he had moved. I could hear, faintly at first, a tiny shove on the door. Within a minute yes, another push... and then another... and another. The door still wasn't opening, but it was slowly loosening. Jock continued to nudge it on and off for the next little while. Each time he pushed at the door I looked up from my work and I could see the door giving way a little more. He continued to press his weight on the door from the other side.

By this time I was fully engaged, not on my work but on how long he would spend trying to get in the room and would his patience be rewarded?

One more push I kept thinking as I stayed quiet behind the door. *One more time!*

Eventually, after many attempts, the door suddenly gave way and opened into the room along with a little ginger cat following.

A pink nose, a set of whiskers appeared and then two green eyes looked round the door at me. He stood still, his stare meeting mine. He regarded me for a moment and then turned and left the room.

He joined the dog in the sun and was still there when I left for work. I will never understand the ways of a cat!

Never ever, ever give up.

There are things in our life which take a huge amount of patience and effort. Whether you're praying or hoping, working towards an exam or saving for a mortgage. Whether you are recuperating from an illness or recovering from a divorce or bereavement.

Little by little, day by day, add to what you have already done and together it will compound into something which moves you towards your goal. Whether you are searching for peace in a nightmare or catching up on a backlog of papers, as we put one foot in front of another and take each moment as it comes, we move forward.

Never give up.

Whatever I have, wherever I am, I can make it through anything in the One who makes me who I am.

Philippians 4:13

Notes:

Chapter 7

Papa and the Cat

We were on holiday in Shetland, house sitting for some good friends. Looking after their church, we were able to spend the week relaxing and enjoying some of the pleasures of The Shetland Isles.

We fell in love with the island some years ago while celebrating Kevin's fortieth birthday there and have visited, either to minister or socialise ever since.

Days there for us began with a lazy breakfast, then a drive around the island, lunch out, maybe a walk along an isolated beach with seals swimming alongside us, reading in the afternoon and a leisurely meal back at base in the evening. Our friends' life, running a busy church on the island, was far from like that but for us, it was a welcome break away from the busyness of our pastorate in the city of Glasgow.

Their house stood halfway up a steep street which rose from the main paved thoroughfare through the centre of Lerwick. Shops lined both sides of the road and I always enjoyed meandering through the collection of gift stores and cafes.

Our main reason for staying on that occasion was not just to house sit but to stay with Papa, their cat. This involved feeding him twice a day then waiting twenty minutes while he sat on the doorstep deciding whether to stay in or go out. This particular morning, after a particularly long decision making process, he finally made the decision to stay in the house.

Some while later, I could hear the strangest sound emitting from the dining room which overlooked the street. On entering I saw an enraged Papa on the inside of the window and another cat on the outside of the glass. Both cats were in full combat mode, trying to fight each other with the glass in between. Papa, at that moment, fur standing on end, looked remarkably like a toilet brush!

Without waiting I rushed up to Papa to pull him away and he turned, spit, hissed and what I can only say, emitted a low growling sound, snarled and then roared at me with a fury I have never seen from a cat. I'd never heard so many different sounds coming out of this one, usually delightful little cat! I've since read that cats make more than one hundred different sounds and I think at that moment, I heard most of them!

I can't tell you how quickly I left that room and slammed the door behind me. It was several hours before I dare let him out and only then after I had prepared my escape route before flinging the door open and running!

But a cursory glance seemed to show that he was now back to the happy Papa we knew and loved, having seen the cat off that morning and relaxed in the sunny windowsill for the rest of the day.

Nevertheless, I spent the rest of the week walking round the edge of any room he was in and making sure there was plenty of food in his bowl just in case he felt like eating a medium sized pastor's wife from Glasgow.

Papa and the Cat

There's definitely an art in waiting.

Devalued, in a day of activity, action and assertiveness, waiting is a forgotten art. They say "fools jump in where angels fear to tread" and many a crisis is made worse by our inability to step back and wait.

In waiting to speak or to act we gain precious time to think, to observe and to understand. We gain space to see the real issues and grasp the whole picture. We get wisdom to know the best words to say and the wise moves to make.

Knowing when to purposefully step back isn't weakness. It's a strength and it's a skill which will enhance your life and your experience.

Do you know when to wait? Do you know when to stand back and allow time to do its invaluable work?

**Hot tempers start fights;
a calm, cool spirit keeps the peace.**

Proverbs 15:18

Notes:

Little Thoughts from Great Cats

Chapter 8

Plenty of Purrs

Taking Jock to the vets wasn't my favourite occupation due to my inability to actually get the cat into the cat carrier! In fact I had nearly missed several appointments due to Jock's determination not to go to the vet. He definitely regarded each visit as a kind of torture chamber of being prodded and poked in any available orifice the man in the white coat may select. Nevertheless, this time it was really necessary.

I wasn't happy leaving Jock at the vets as we left for the ministry trip. I wanted to be on hand to find out what was wrong and to take him home again as soon as I could. I kept in touch by phone with my neighbour, between meetings. He still wasn't eating, he was sleeping and drinking very little. She even offered to go to the vets and feed him by hand while we were away.

We arrived back at the vet's office on the Monday afternoon to a sombre looking professional.

"Feline Leukaemia?" I repeated "What's that?"

The vet explained. Feline Leukaemia is passed from cat to cat through transfer of saliva, blood or urine when cats groom or fight and eighty five per cent of cats die within three years. Some a lot sooner.

We talked some more and learned that if Jock recovered, which was doubtful, he would never be allowed outside again, thus preventing him passing on the virus to other cats and catching other infections himself.

"You can take him home," the vet said, "but I advise you leave him here, he is very sick."

I chose to take him home and in my mind began to devise a recovery plan. It was more than I could hope for, but I would try.

At first, he ate nothing but after a few days, he began to eat a tiny bit of chicken and within two weeks, was eating a full plate. Plenty of laying on of hands in prayer and twenty five purrs a day, I had planned.

Cats purr, not just when they are happy but also when they are ill or distressed but it's a self soothing action of self healing which I thought would do the cat no harm. To start with, I could pray but I couldn't get any purrs from him at all. Then I got one, and I knew I could get more! And I did. Not many at first but slowly they multiplied! We continued the prayer and the purrs too and over the months, we watched the blood test results rise.

Jock lived for several years and although he never again ran over the fields of freedom, he certainly had a great time purring!!

What do you like to do? Not because you need to or you must but simply because you like to?

So often the tasks of daily life crowd out those activities we do simply for pleasure.

They can include social interaction with others. They can involve mastery of a new skill or extending your creativity. It can be the pure enjoyment of reading a book, watching a film or walking a dog. It can be something physical like gardening, rambling or dancing.

A lack of money, time, energy or health may dictate what we choose to some extent. But enjoyable things make us more productive in our daily lives.

Why not think carefully about what you enjoy today? God has created you to experience abundant life.

**A right time to cry and another to laugh,
A right time to lament and another to cheer.**

Ecclesiastes 3:4

Notes:

Chapter 9

Sunrise

At least once every holiday, when we stay in Lanzarote, we go and watch the sunrise. I have to admit, I would never be the one to suggest it, but having done it, I wouldn't miss it for the world.

Walking through the deserted streets, we pass an odd car on the way to work or a lone cleaner, preparing a bar for the day's tourists but other than that the streets are deserted. Very soon, we make our way up hill to the cliff tops which look down over the Spanish resort.

Lights are coming on all over the town in the hundreds of little white properties upon which we look down. Fishing boats make their way over the darkened water to the port below and begin to unload their night's catch.

All buildings are white and no more than two or three floors at the most in Lanzarote, a legacy of the architect Cesar Manrique. It makes for a Bethlehem kind of scene as the white houses stretch up the hill.

All is quiet, it seems that no one knows we're up here. No one that is except the cats. There are many wild cats in Lanzarote but they are wisely encouraged into certain areas of the resort. They are neutered, kept healthy and fed. And one of these areas is the clifftop from which we watch daybreak. Sometimes there are tiny kittens there too, spending their days playing and learning their skills for hunting and fishing.

Pretty soon after our arrival, in fact seconds, eight or ten cats arrive to see what we have brought them to eat. Black, Siamese, tabby and ginger they arrive one by one and patiently sit and wait for the cat biscuits to appear. White Tip, a coal black cat with just a white tip to his tail comes especially close until a Siamese with a tabby face and paws, pushes him out of the way.

After we have watched the horizon change from black to yellow to orange to pink then baby blue, we wander down along the boardwalk and on the way, pass the next cat sanctuary, beautiful long haired Siamese's, jet black tomcats and occasionally again, tiny little kittens. Many of them, just settling down for the morning after a night catching mice, fish and other delicacies. Several of them make their way towards us but the grey cat, eyes closed doesn't even stir. He no doubt, opened his eyes a couple of weeks or so after birth and has not opened them much since! He has obviously had a good night and has eaten his fill. He adjusts himself a little and snuggles even further into the cleft of the rock as the increasing heat of the sun shines down.

Cats sweat through their paw pads, having no other sweat glands in their body and looking at them all there, I found it amazing that by the time the temperature reached its usual 30 degrees in the heat of the afternoon, they would still be lying in the sun looking as cool as ever.

Those paw pads must be working overtime!

Are there times you feel the heat of the sun? Times when events or situations of life just seem a little too hot to handle?

Do you have a cleft of a rock into which you can position yourself and take shelter from the sun or the storm? Everyone needs a cleft in a rock, where we gain spiritual strength to face the world once again.

A rock never moves, whatever the weather. It is something we can depend on to be unchanging, always be the same, surrounding us above, below, to our left and right and behind.

But the way ahead is not blocked. It is open ready for us to move ahead when the time is right. Until then it is cool and shaded, away from the heat of the day.

Do you feel the heat of the sun? Do you need to find the shelter of Almighty God today?

You who sit down in the High God's presence,
spend the night in Shaddai's shadow,
Say this:
God, you're my refuge.
I trust in you and I'm safe!

Psalm 91:1-2

Notes:

Chapter 10

Mickey

Mickey was miserable. At least she looked it – if cats can look miserable, my friend said. Her coat was dull and although she spent hours grooming herself it never looked good. And when she wasn't cleaning herself, she was having kittens! She kept having to move them around to safe places – she was a very good mum! Producing between one and nine of these small bundles of fur regularly from the age of four months, she definitely deserved a break. She had been called Mickey as her owners had assumed she was a male – before the kittens began arriving – and the name stuck. They called her babies "micklets"!

My friend, Mary, lived in Uganda and the feline seemed to live in the grounds of the house next door. The beauty of the country and the wonderful hot sun was irrelevant to this pet. In fact, she couldn't even be called a pet, she was merely a vermin catcher and a kitten machine.

One day my friend had an idea. Why not offer to pay for half the cost of neutering the little creature? She wasn't sure if the owner would agree but the sight of the little cat was heartrending. So the deal was done and following the next litter of kittens, my friend called her vet who came and spayed Mickey on the verandah. The whole thing was watched – and – videoed, by the neighbour's intrigued children.

After the operation, my friend looked after her on her side of the fence and in a few days the little cat was running about as normal, except that she liked it more in this house. So she stayed. Life was definitely better for her on that side of the fence.

And so she settled in with my friend, and Honey, a stray dog who'd also found life better in Mary's house. She was quite able to stand up for herself when she needed to, having lived a tough life on the other side of the fence. Very soon the cat and dog became devoted to each other and when my friend finished her work in Uganda, the dilemma was huge. Should she send the pets to the streets to fend for themselves? I so hoped not, but it was not my decision to make.

Two months later, I received a photo. There were Mickey and Honey sunning themselves on a verandah in Derbyshire.

"We arrived home yesterday..." wrote Mary "...and they act as though they've been here all their lives! Mickey has already adopted the taps in the bathroom as her own personal drinking fountain!"

Two very blessed little animals I am sure…

Mickey

Has anyone ever rescued you?

We read of hostages freed, families in fires, rescued, and workers trapped in a lift, released. Doctors, prisons and rehabilitation centres rescue people from imprisonment of the mind. Prayer or counselling can rescue people from past hurts which affect their daily actions or reactions, and pastors and other Christians can point us to God's peace and rest, and so release us from turmoil in difficult times.

When someone rescues us, they point us to freedom and release us from those things which prevented that freedom. They change our circumstances and help us move forward into new things. We can be rescued from a problem with advice, rescued from poverty with aid or rescued from loneliness with company.

Has anyone rescued you? Never forget them. Why not write and thank them today?

Make sure you're firmly on His side of the fence!

I've been carrying you on my back
from the day you were born,
And I'll keep on carrying you
when you're old.
I'll be there, bearing you when
you're old and grey.
I've done it and will keep on doing it,
carrying you on my back, saving you.

Isaiah 46:3b-4

Notes:

Chapter 11

Night Music

The sun was hot, the sky was blue and there was I, practicing my scales!

Our piano was in the back living room and I could see the green grass of the large lawn, the white apple blossom and the beautiful pink array of the flowering cherry which overhung from Bridget's garden next door. It all beckoned me outside. But my piano exam was the next Tuesday and I turned away and began to play *C sharp harmonic minor* once again.

When Porky first saw my piano he was intrigued. Hearing, being the strongest of his senses, he could recognise the softest of sounds. Sometimes he would move his ears independently as much as 180 degrees as he suddenly woke from a sleep, listening intently to sounds I could not hope to hear. I knew he had excellent hearing.

I thought he would be afraid of the piano once he heard its sound but he seemed all the keener to jump on the stool and explore. Soon he was sitting on the top of the open lid watching the hammers as they hit the strings and fell back to their place. He would try and grab them with his paws, at times almost overbalancing into the piano.

It was a dark night in winter when I awoke with a start. It was 2am. I could hear a noise. I sat up in bed and listened. Nothing. I lay back down and began to drift off into sleep. There it was again. Music. Scary music! The lowest notes of the piano were sounding themselves! I silently swung my legs out of bed and tiptoed to the door. There it was again. Hardly breathing I made my way downstairs and stood at the living room door.

I stared. There in front of me was Porky walking up and down the piano keys, purring and gazing at the cat biscuits left on the table, as though they would obediently fall out of the box to the sound of his music. I remembered offering him biscuits as a reward to play the keys the previous day which he refused to do.

Now, hungry at 2am, he was simply asking to eat!

Many nights after that, I would hear his music. Except when I remembered to shut the lid!

Do you like night time or do you dread it?

At night our bodies are silent and still and it is the time when we reward them with rest in order that they can serve us well tomorrow. We put our responsibilities aside and we dream and take ourselves into new worlds.

Without night, we would never see the stars. A night sky full of stars is a gift to behold. Look up in the daytime and you see nothing. Raise your eyes at night and it can be breathtaking.

At night, in the safety of our bed we lose consciousness and our thoughts rest. Some nights are good and maybe at times, some are not, but morning always comes.

Feeling lonely or having a head full of thoughts or worry occasionally is a negative experience of being human. When we spend our days productively, night can be a haven of rest. There is silent music in the night if you search for it.

Why not begin each night from now on with a prayer of thanks to God for the good things in your life? Set each night on course to be truly renewing for tomorrow.

You'll take afternoon naps without a worry,
You'll enjoy a good night's sleep.
No need to panic over alarms or surprises,
or predictions that doomsday's just around
the corner,
Because God will be right there with you;
He'll keep you safe and sound.

Proverbs 3:24-26

Notes:

Chapter 12

The Adventures of Andrew

Andrew is naturally nocturnal. No one has ever trained him to be any other way.

He keeps the mice population absent and in return he gets board and lodgings, and plenty of food. He sleeps all day in some quiet corner of the Lanzarote complex and gets up around tea time. Visiting apartments one by one for his daily dinners, leaving bits on the plate to collect later through the night, he must work hard to stay so slim!

One day I found him standing at the door of the bathroom peering in with interest. Kevin suggested that he might be wondering why we kept our 'litter tray' right next to our 'cleaning gear' as no self-respecting cat would ever do that. I doubt he was.

As with all our cats, he has his own secret, private life. Those who fit webcams to their animal's collar to watch their nocturnal wanderings often get a big surprise at their adventures as we sleep. Their nocturnal eyes searching out rodents, lizards and other small creatures, all fair game to be caught in order to consume their necessary intake of protein. Their ears which hear five times stronger than ours, able to hear the tiny squeak of a mouse or the rustle of a bat's wing. Their nose with a sense of smell fourteen times stronger than ours, searching out food, or other cats or their own marked territory.

Andrew could fit through the tiniest gaps imaginable and as long as his head would go through, he knew he was ok! His thick soft pads made him almost silent as he sneaked up on his prey. His eighteen claws extended to help him climb the highest fence, he would then have to jump down, or climb down backwards to get to the floor once more.

I saw Andrew one night. I heard him run across the roof, jump down and then I watched him from the window. He was perched on a wall just staring intently in one spot. I could see nothing. (Although cats can't see in complete darkness, they have powerful night vision and need six times less light than their human owner does). He waited a while and then jumped down. He began striding from door to door as though he were in charge of the world, pacing the floor, guarding against any little mouse which may dare to cross his path.

Gone was the purring, gentle cat rubbing itself round our legs. Ears alert, glowing eyes reflecting the light, treading stealthily as though he were a tiger... I'm sure in his mind, he was!

There are things happening all around us which we rarely appreciate. Just because you don't see it doesn't mean it's not there.

Things to enjoy like sunsets and autumn colours and a deep blue sky. Sounds to hear like the roll of thunder, the crash of waves and the cry of a seagull. There are things to feel like the falling of rain, the snow on our skin and the softness of a pet's fur. There are tastes to experience from our favourite meal, to the salt on the sea air and a cool drink in the heat of summer. There are scents to acknowledge like wood smoke in the evening, the grass after the rain and the bark of a tree.

So many of these things surround us but are never acknowledged.

Why not awaken those senses today and appreciate once more those things you did as a child...

God's whole creation is living and breathing all around you.

> **But the basic reality of God is plain enough. Open your eyes and there it is! By taking a long and thoughtful look at what God has created, people have always been able to see what their eyes as such can't see: eternal power, for instance, and the mystery of his divine being.**
>
> *Romans 1:19-20a*

Notes:

Chapter 13

The Windowsill

It was a cloudy morning when the double glazing company arrived to replace our windows. We had planned to change them when we first moved into the house as the existing ones were old and draughty. But with one thing and another, four years had passed before we improved our upstairs four in a block flat with brand new windows.

The windowsill was always a favourite place for Jock to hang out. That cat definitely had a degree in comfort and he was quite apt to choose the most inconvenient place in the house with remarkable regularity. Even though he had a *state of the art* cat basket in the living room complete with matching blankets and a toy mouse should he need company, there was always somewhere else he preferred to be: on top of the wardrobe, in front of the fire, looking out of the floor to ceiling window onto the golf course or at the top of the stairs waiting for JF to call for him.

The outside sill of the front window was especially favourite for he could watch the cars, people and cats passing by on the street below, enjoy the sun and fresh air while at the same time have access to get back in whenever he wanted.

It was a wide windowsill with ample room to turn round at the end and make his way back into the bedroom whenever he wished. He would spend hours there, watching the world go by.

The day of the upgrade went very smoothly and by nightfall the new windows were installed looking very smart and shiny, and I then took time to polish them up and arrange new ornaments on the inside windowsills.

The next morning, as usual I made the bed and opened the window to air the bedroom. I left for work at lunchtime, as I did admiring our new windows with Jock sitting inside looking out.

"Where's Jock?" I asked Kevin on my return after school.

"He loves the new windows, he's been sitting outside for hours on the windowsill," he replied.

I entered the bedroom to see our cat standing on the outside sill, at that moment attempting to turn round but unable to manoeuvre his body one hundred and eighty degrees on the new slim sill. No wonder he'd been out all day. He couldn't get in again!

I walked towards the window only to see Jock suddenly unbalance off the edge of the sill, fall and land right beside a startled JF. Amazingly cats have the ability to fall from a great height, right themselves in the air and still land on their feet (apparently due to a reflex between their eyes and some balance organs in their inner ear, telling it where it is in the air).

Even so, thank goodness it was only one floor I thought, looking down on Jock and his brother, who had a very surprised look on his face!

The Windowsill

Have things ever changed in your life for the worst? You weren't expecting it, you didn't plan for it but one day, you awoke to find out that life as you had known it had changed? Maybe a redundancy, maybe an illness, maybe a death, maybe a financial crisis.

From time to time life throws us a curved ball and the day to day life which we enjoyed in the sun is no longer stretching out before us in the way we always knew it. Things which we took for granted, which we thought would always be around are gone, and for a while it seems we have nowhere to turn.

But life is full of new beginnings and strange as it may seem after a winter, there is always a spring. That is the pattern of life.

Tiny frail buds to begin with but as they grow and become established, new life begin to reveal itself to us and we find that although the clouds have obscured the sun, the clouds can't stop the sun from shining. Sometimes it feels like God is far away but in time we realise He has been with us all the time.

Why not acknowledge that fact today about the difficult days in your life?

> Be strong. Take courage. Don't be intimidated. Don't give them a second thought because God, your God, is striding ahead of you. He's right there with you. He won't let you down; he won't leave you.
>
> *Deuteronomy 31:6*

Notes:

Little Thoughts from Great Cats

Chapter 14

The Party

"**H**appy birthday to youuuuuuuuuuuuuu..."

I sang at the top of my voice bursting into rapturous applause to end the song, along with the table full of nine year olds who sat alongside me. I eyed the cat in the corner of the room, which sat there staring at me. The cutting of the birthday cake came next and we excitedly waited for our piece to be carefully placed in front of us. It was a pink iced cake and belonged to my best friend Lynne.

I sat quietly for a moment, enjoying the taste of the soft sponge and of course saving the icing until last. As I did, out of the corner of my eye, I checked on the cat. Sukie was still looking at me. Still sitting in the same place.

After the cake came jelly and ice cream.

"Me, me, me, me..." we chanted in unison in answer to someone's question *who's going to be first?* To me, jelly and ice cream was the best. Better than sandwiches and crisps... and even birthday cake. Especially red jelly.

Eventually, I laid down my spoon and licked my lips, unable to resist a peak at the cat who had settled on all fours, but even now never taking her eyes off mine. *Easier to spring at a moment's notice,* I thought as I shifted uneasily in my chair.

After the food, we played more party games. I declined being blindfolded for *Pin the Tail on the Donkey* so I could keep an eye on the furry creature in the corner but I joined in all the rest.

At last it was time to go home and we put on our coats and said *goodbye* as mums queued down the hall to take away their offspring.

"The cat kept staring at me..." I volunteered to my mum as I held her hand and hurried home.

"He was probably looking at all of you... feeling sorry about your disabilities..." joked my mum. "...no tails, only two legs, no whiskers, ears that don't move and no fur to puff out. I'm sure he was just concerned for you all..."

"No, he kept staring at *ME*..." I worriedly assured her.

"Were you looking at the cat?"

"A bit... not much..."

"Well, cats sometimes stare to resolve conflict..." my mum continued, "... it's always best to look away or blink, not to stare back as it's a sort of aggressive action... it makes him uncomfortable."

"It was a girl," I muttered under my breath and then forgot about the cat.

Late that night as I lay in my bed, my friend's words, before the party, returned to me: *She's a nice cat, but if she stares at you, there's no telling what she'll do... don't look at her whatever you do...!*

Relieved to have survived, I snuggled further down under the covers.

But then again, there was always next time…!

HAPPY BIRTHDAY!

Are there distractions in your life? So often, we can take our eye off the main issue. Many things can distract us from focusing on the most important thing in life.

A man can be distracted by his work over his family. A mother can be distracted by problems rather than enjoying the gift of her child. A university student can become distracted from her study by the social whirl of the current scene. A child can be distracted from his lessons by bullies. A senior citizen can be distracted from a fulfilling life by loneliness.

We can also be distracted by regret of past mistakes, by possessions, money or pleasure, by the need for perfection or the pull of tomorrow's excitement. There are hundreds of distractions to take our mind away from the task we have been given to do.

Every day is a gift of God and the only 'this day' we will have. Will you make the most of every moment and rejoice in the small pleasures of today?

> **Oh listen, dear child –**
> **become wise;**
> **point your life in the right direction.**
>
> *Proverbs 23:19*

Notes:

Little Thoughts from Great Cats

Chapter 15

The Ottoman

There were so many things going on that Friday. I had finished school for the holidays and rushed home to throw some things into the case ready for our trip down south. In the spare room, pushing the cat from off the ottoman I lifted the lid and removed some blankets that I had promised Kevin's mum next time we visited.

Jock resettled himself on the open lid and closed his eyes once again. He may be my little cat asleep in the room but I knew that in his dreams he would soon be that raging tiger in the mountains! I left the room to put the kettle on and then spent the rest of the evening sorting out the packing and marking my final few books before preparing my school bag for after the holidays.

The next day was bright and sunny as I tidied round before we left. I went from room to room straightening cushions, closing cupboards and checking windows.

"It's strange Jock's not back in," Kevin commented.

Jock always arrived back early morning and was usually waiting outside our upstairs door to get in for his breakfast, before joining Mary and I on our morning walk. He was no doubt somewhere about, I thought, cleaning his paws and ears and legs and no doubt spending the usual inordinate amount of time on his bottom (…though second thoughts, he did that when our visitors were here two evenings ago!). Today he was nowhere to be seen and Mary and I had walked without him.

I began to wonder where he was. I searched the house, scoured the garden and looked from our window over the golf course. I rang Suzanne to see if JF was around. He had arrived home as usual, early morning and she hadn't seen Jock anywhere.

"We'll have to leave," Kevin said "and let Alison know when she comes, that he's still out." I wandered back to the window to look once more over the golf course and as I did I thought, just thought, I heard a very faint meow.

"I can hear him," I said to Kevin, but when we listened further we heard nothing. I began to move towards the door again and as I did, I heard it again.

"I know he's here."

The meow was so faint I knew it could have almost been in my imagination. I listened and listened. It sounded almost like he was inside the walls of the house, it was so far away.

Once I knew he was somewhere in the house, there was no way I was leaving. We hunted and hunted and even looked in the attic, but every time we seemed to get close, the meows went away once more.

Adult cats only meow to communicate with humans. They will spit, purr and hiss at other cats but they work hard on this method of human communication, and even change their meows in order to manipulate their owner. Jock's meow sounded faint but desperate. We continued to search but I could find no place that the meows became louder.

"Where did you see him last?" Kevin asked eventually. *Where was he?* I thought.

And then I knew.

I rushed to the ottoman in the spare room which was now closed with a pile of ironing on top. I quickly threw opened the lid. Inside was a very comfortable little cat who had made his bed on the remaining blankets at the bottom before getting shut inside. Was I glad to see him?

It definitely was the last time I ever shut the ottoman without checking!

A good example of something that was lost and was found? But there are also times when we lose but we never find. These can be very painful times.

Losing possessions or money can be traumatic but in time, moving on is usually not too difficult. When we lose people or for some, even animals, the process is much more painful.

We can lose because of death or divorce or the end of a relationship, not something anyone wants to endure. And these things set us back, sometimes for months or years but during that time they also create within us qualities which improve us as people.

Losing someone can show us what really matters in life. It can help us to be truly empathetic with people who follow us through similar situations to our own and it can show us who our true friends are. It can give us certainty after a period of uncertainty and it can force us in time to move forward into new days and moments. It can help us appreciate the fact that time is precious and every moment counts.

Are you making the losses in your life work for you?

He comes alongside us when we go
through hard times, and before you know
it, he brings us alongside someone else who
is going through hard times so that we can
be there for that person just as God was
there for us.

2 Corinthians 1:4-5

Notes:

Little Thoughts from Great Cats

Chapter 16

Moving House

Porky loved the house we lived in. It was all he had known. Since a tiny kitten, he had played in the orchard, run up and down the lawn and lay sleeping in the sun on those hot sunny days. He would enjoy full bowls of his favourite food and look accusingly at any bowl only half full, as if we were trying to starve him.

And then everything changed.

It was a year to the day before our wedding day and my parents had sold us their house and I was moving with them for one year into their bungalow before we married. I went to school that morning to teach my Primary 3 class and returned home to a new house.

Everyone liked the move but for Porky, gone were the adventures in the orchard and the territory he had always known. Cats he had grown up with disappeared overnight and he was now faced with being the *new boy on the block.* Different cats ruled, all with territory of their own, marked out for months or even years.

Where was the concrete slab on which he slept away many an afternoon? What? No lawn to dig up? No upstairs floor either where he could look down on the world, one of his favourite pastimes. Wherever had his life gone?

Porky was kept in the new bungalow for the next couple of weeks and then was allowed out to explore his new territory. All went well for the first month. And then he disappeared!

Day after day, night after night, no Porky. Quite often, lost cats have the ability to find their way home. Scientists think it's to do with the angle of sunlight or even magnetised cells in their brains which act as a compass, but I wasn't sure that Porky knew where he lived any more.

I was worried! What would he do without his favourite blue saucer to eat off? He loved that. He wasn't fussy – he just liked to eat his dinner off his blue saucer!

We regularly checked back at the old house although it was a couple of miles away but three weeks later when Porky hadn't returned, we felt he was gone for good.

It was three o'clock in the morning when I heard the door knocker sound. We didn't have a cat flap but we did have a letterbox with a knocker at floor height in both our former and our new home. That was Porky's way of getting in at night and my bedroom was right at the end of the hall. I shot out of bed. I could see his little frame through the glass. I opened the door and Porky strolled up the hall as though he'd never been away. Was he hungry? No. Where'd he been? No idea!

We gave him gourmet cat food the next night as a celebration. Big mistake! Suddenly he didn't like the cheap cat food he'd consumed for the last ten years. Amazingly the taste had changed overnight! So, gourmet it became. Every cloud has a silver lining.

For a cat.

Have you ever stepped out of your comfort zone?

There are occasions we choose to do that and there are periods in life that we are forced by circumstances to do so.

Familiarity and similarity help us feel safe and secure but situations which are new and uncomfortable help us to grow. When we pass through an unfamiliar place be it physically, mentally or emotionally, it feels strange and the terrain is unknown but it can birth within us new strengths that we lack.

Settling long term can sometimes bring apathy but challenges in life bring just that – life! There is a life outside your comfort zone and before long, that which was so strange becomes the new normal.

A comfort zone is a different thing to different people. It is personal to you! A new job, a new friend, a new home, a new country? A new life situation, a new holiday, a new role, a new restaurant?

Life is a set of changes whether enforced or chosen and once we embrace them, we find a new perspective of life.

Are there changes which you need to make?

I'll show up and take care of you as I promised and bring you back home. I know what I'm doing. I have it all planned out – plans to take care of you, not abandon you, plans to give you the future you hope for. When you call on me, when you come and pray to me, I'll listen.

Jeremiah 29:10b-12

Notes:

Chapter 17

The Birds

Mary the dog was settled next to Jock on the rug in front of the fire. Both were sleeping. I whispered Mary's name softly and in an instant she was by my side, gazing up expectantly, tail wagging. I called Jock's name out loud. Not a movement. Not a whisker twitch. Without doubt, he would recognise my voice but was far too 'cool' to acknowledge it. No doubt he would consider, that to respond to us would only encourage us to do it more. He continued to appear to sleep!

The experts say that Jock remembers things for sixteen hours and Mary for only five minutes! I had no idea who remembered what!

Although they lived in the same home, that was the only similarity that I could see between them.

Jock would push at an ornament on a shelf to see if it would bounce. He would enjoy a tummy rub but only so much so, before he bit your finger or clawed your hand. Mary would lie forever for a tummy rub any time of day or night, flat on her back paws outstretched for maximum effect, and things stayed on the shelf where you put them (usually).

Mary wagged her tail when she was happy, Jock when he was cross. Mary loved to be part of the pack and really pined if she were left alone for long. Jock was an individual and believed that he was *leader* of the pack. He would look disdainfully at us as we came home from work at the end of the day, obviously annoyed that we had invaded his peace.

The greatest difference was the *dog chocolate* factor. Jock, as with all cats, couldn't taste sweet things and would never offer to do so. Mary, on the other hand, would camp out for a month if she caught a whiff of chocolate in the fridge!

I must admit that Jock's habit of appearing to watch something or someone move across the room that neither I nor Mary could see, could sometimes be more than a little un-nerving!

Mary would sleep on our bed while Jock toured the streets and fields at nighttime searching for some little treasure to leave us on the doormat. One morning, I opened the front door to see Jock running at top speed towards our house pursued by a huge flock of low flying squawking birds. *I wonder what he's been up to,* I thought. I didn't ask!

If the theories were true that Jock remembered things for sixteen hours and Mary for only five minutes I think *that* might be one occasion when Jock would prefer the memory of a dog!

Cats are cats and dogs are dogs. And people are people. But just as every face and fingerprint is different, so too are we different in many other ways.

You are totally unique not better, not worse, but unique. Your temperament, character and personality are unique. Your attributes, strengths and gifts are unique. Your preferences, passions and dislikes are unique.

Whether, through generation or environment, you are you and you were created to be you. I've heard it said that one of the blessings of getting older is that you begin to know yourself (how and why you react as you do) and to feel comfortable in your own skin.

Why not begin to celebrate the person God created you to be and maybe for the first time – say to yourself and the world "This is me!" God made you to be you!

With his assistance why not be the very best 'you' that you can be?

You know me inside and out, you know every bone in my body;

You know exactly how I was made, bit by bit, how I was sculpted from nothing into something.

Like an open book, you watched me grow from conception to birth; all the stages of my life were spread out before you,

The days of my life all prepared before I'd even lived one day.

Psalm 139:15-16

Notes:

Little Thoughts from Great Cats

Chapter 18

The Papa Stour Kitten

I sat behind the sand dune, sheltered from the slight wind looking down onto the beach at Sandness. We had rented a cottage in a tiny hamlet on the west coast of Shetland. Never having been there before, we were continually overawed by the experience. It was a place where the grandeur of nature overcame all else.

We had stood at the top of rocky cliffs overlooking crashing waves, we watched the sun set into the sea night after night and saw the puffins nesting in the cliffs.

We had made some good friends in Lerwick too and enjoyed fun and fellowship at a local church there. We wandered down the paved shopping street and watched the ferries sail back and forth from Aberdeen. To us, it was a wonderful place.

I looked down from my sand dune and studied the beach. We had seen two otters during our first few days. They were playing where the sea met the sand and looked like two puppies enjoying each other's company. I thought viewing otters might be an everyday occurrence, not realising it was a rarity.

I was amazed at the rhythm of the beach as I watched it throughout our days there. Everything happened at the same time each day. The arctic turns pattering about near the sea, the ducks followed by their tiny ducklings and the seals swimming alongside us as we walked along the sand each day.

Today was different for we were going to choose a kitten. Not for us but with our friends. A litter had been born on Papa Stour, a tiny island off the coast of Shetland. At that time Papa Stour, an island of caves, stacks, arches, cliffs and blowholes was the home of twenty-five or so people plus a variety of otters, killer whales, seals and porpoises. And now a new litter of kittens.

The ferry would take forty-five minutes to get there but we were going on a small motor boat owned by a Papa Stour resident and that afternoon we boarded the little boat and crossed the water.

An hour later, we were making our way into a barn and viewed four tiny kittens nestled in the hay. Our friends looked at them all in turn and chose the most handsome ball of fur we had ever seen.

Born on Papa Stour, what would he be called? No question at all. 'Papa' of course.

Joy can be found in the most surprising of places! An unexpected day off, a favourite holiday, an early morning walk, quality time with a friend, children's laughter, the embrace of our family, the devotion of a pet, the photos of loved ones, the sound of our favourite melodies and songs, a phone call or text from far away...

And when we focus on the experiences we find pleasurable things begin to happen to us! Scientists tell us that what we think and feel, both good and bad, affect our body, shape our outlook and we know that so often our outlook can shape our life.

There is so much joy to discover in everyday life and it can often be found in the most surprising places!

Could you begin to discover more today?

Feast there in the Presence of God, your God. Celebrate everything that you and your families have accomplished under the blessing of God, your God.

Deuteronomy 12:7

Notes:

Chapter 19

Golly the Goldfish

I was fourteen years old and I wanted another goldfish.

"Aren't you a bit old for goldfish now?" enquired my mum, more than once. I'd often had goldfish but never with a cat in the house. Jock our beloved dog had lived for ten years with numerous goldfish but he had gone to the kennel in the sky months ago and a new pack leader was in town! Porky the cat now ruled supreme.

Nevertheless Golly the Goldfish number six arrived one sunny afternoon and was carefully placed in his round bowl in my bedroom. We had discussed various options for the bowl and all agreed this was probably the most sensible place for him to live. I can quite understand how cats get confused when we store a bird or a fish in a cage or a bowl for years, never seem to do anything with it and then get very cross when they happen to eat it one day. But Porky would have boundaries, of which the bedroom door was one!

All went well and bedroom doors were closed before leaving the house, at least for a while. Even on the occasion I left my door ajar, I returned to Golly happily swimming round in his bowl with Porky the cat sunning himself downstairs, oblivious to who lived on the top floor.

It was one Saturday, we went on a trip to my uncle and aunt's returning in the late afternoon. Mum wanted to call at the shop for a loaf of bread but dad wanted to get home for *Dr Who*. They had a little conversation and Dad won so we went straight home.

Dad opened the front door and who should be at the top of the stairs but Porky the cat.

"What's wrong with the cat?" I asked. He seemed to be playing with his little orange toy. Dad looked up the stairs and suddenly, faster than I had ever seen him move before, ran upstairs two at a time. Quick as a flash, he pushed the cat down the stairs and bent to scoop up the little orange toy in his hands. Before I even realised what was taking place Golly the Goldfish was back in his bowl swimming round with a most surprised look on his face.

(Come to think of it he always looked pretty surprised).

"Well that was one of his nine lives gone," said my dad.

"I thought that was a cat, not a fish?" I said.

"Whatever, that is one very blessed little fish..." replied Dad.

And he sat down in his favourite armchair just as the Daleks entered the room.

I say God bless *Dr Who*!

Golly the Goldfish

Do you appreciate that someone is looking out for you?

When you were, or if you are, still on a journey towards knowing God, it seemed / seems impossible that there could be a real person who created and sustained the universe who could be interested in your life.

Our concept of God is often dependent on our earthly father and this sometimes makes it very difficult to see God as He really is.

In addition to this, it's hard to understand why God doesn't always do what we want. It can be very tough when He allows circumstances to move away from what would be our first choice.

But whoever you are, wherever you stand in your journey of faith, He is looking out for you today, always working things for the best whatever it may seem at the time.

Why not thank Him for that and keep in your thoughts that He is looking out for you today?

> **God guards you from every evil, he guards your very life. He guards you when you leave and when you return, he guards you now, he guards you always.**
>
> *Psalm 121:7-8*

Notes:

Little Thoughts from Great Cats

Chapter 20

Boardwalk Fishing

We wandered slowly along the boardwalk. The mountains in the distance were dark against the bright blue sky. The sun was hot on our backs.

The boardwalk was a wonderful place to be. Ducks with ducklings in their wake, fish in abundance of all sizes and a cat sanctuary amongst the rocks halfway along the walkway. We stopped as always to look at the cats. Some sleeping, some cleaning themselves and one or two restlessly changing their sleeping place in the sun.

At Christmas, here stands a tableau with a stable, a crib and shepherds. There are wooden cows and sheep but there are real cats. And the cats sleep on the stable roof, around the manger and sometimes even nestle in with baby Jesus Himself. Now, that was all gone, just a little straw here and there as a reminder of Christmas.

I stood and looked at the cats. No new chair as their favourite scratching post. No dad taking up too much room on the bed. No personal armchair and no postcard to look forward to from the family's holiday! Nevertheless these cats looked healthy and blissfully happy.

I walked along to the other side of the boardwalk and noticed a movement. Underneath was a little tabby cat by the water's edge. Watching, watching, totally still. The fish in the water seemed to know of his presence as they stayed away from where the little cat stood. We watched some more. Every fibre was poised, eyes sharp and his bent legs at the ready to pounce. We walked round the corner to a seat where we could watch this activity at the water's edge. Each time it seemed he was ready to pounce, he backed off again, his eyes never leaving his dream.

After a while we moved on and walked for a while. On the way back, maybe an hour had passed and we went and sat on that bench once more. The cat was still there, still watching, still waiting, unmoving.

Suddenly he pounced, grabbed the fish and held on tight. Once it stopped struggling, he made his way up the rocks to a safe place to eat his treasure.

From several angles I could see curious cats look up. Some were already making their way towards him. A big black cat stood a few metres away, eyes fixed on the prize. The cat with no tail stood up and all around, cats were waking as they sniffed the air.

I turned to go. I hoped he would enjoy his catch.

But somehow, I doubted it...

Have you ever had anything stolen? It's a very bad experience if you have.

We hear of the theft of cars, possessions, money and even bank accounts being emptied. It seems anything that isn't protected effectively can be taken. And not only the physical... but emotional things too can be stolen from us.

Can people steal our peace or do we surrender it too easily? A mind at peace is a precious thing to possess but one that we must constantly guard with everything we have.

Life happens, circumstances change, time passes, people come and go and the earth continues on its axis. That place of peace which depends not on circumstances is too valuable to let go of.

As problems which would steal your peace surround you, with His help are you willing to do everything you can, to hold onto that gem: peace of heart and peace of mind?

> That's my parting gift to you.
> Peace. I don't leave you the way you're
> used to being left – feeling abandoned,
> bereft. So don't be upset. Don't be
> distraught.
>
> *John 14:27*

Notes:

Chapter 21

Up the Ladder

It was raining and my father was annoyed. He had planned to paint the outside of the house but had opened the curtains that day to grey skies and wet ground.

"Perhaps it will brighten up later," said my mum, forever positive.

Porky looked glum (if cats can look glum) as he stared out of the window, cancelling his day lying in the sun.

Dad had a couple of days off from his job as a TV engineer. Working 9 until 6pm Monday to Saturday included, he had very little time to spare and had planned this for a while. The painting would take a few weeks but today was the day to begin.

Dad was standing at the window and Porky, never one to miss an opportunity, was making the most of the paintbrush-shaped new toys that had just appeared from the shed.

By 11am the sun started to shine and the ground dried up and by noon Dad was setting up his ladder by the bedroom window. He would sand the window frame first and then paint. Balanced on the rungs he carried his sandpaper up to the bedroom window and began work.

I went off to play *Stingray* in the orchard with Michael and Greg. Porky became an alien as he stealthily moved through the long grass.

At 2pm we stopped, Michael and Greg went home and Dad came down the ladder.

All was going well he reported as we sat around eating tomato soup and bread followed by lemon sponge cake for afters. Dad listened to the radio for a while and then gathered up his cloth and paint pot and went off to continue his job.

"Tosh come out here…" he called, using his usual pet name for me. "Tosh!"

I left the room glad of an excuse not to dry the dishes. Dad stood at the bottom of the ladder looking up into the clouds.

"Look there," he said, pointing to the sky. I looked and saw nothing.

"No, not there, there..." he directed. I looked again up to the blue sky, and then I saw him. Right at the top of the ladder. Porky! Always one to get involved in the action. As Dad had come down, Porky had gone up. And with his front paws on the upper rungs and his back paws on the lower ones, he didn't seem to have the know-how to get down. Seeing us below, Porky began to meow loudly.

"I'm sure he can work it out," said my mum, when five minutes later she came out to a very worried Dad and I. But Dad disappeared into the house and a moment later the bedroom window opened from above.

"Much better idea," I shouted as Porky carefully made his way up the remaining few rungs to the safety of the bedroom.

"Perhaps he was looking for the sun?" I suggested.

"Who knows the mind of a cat?" replied my dad as he appeared beside me and climbed the ladder once again.

Have you ever felt at the end of a dead end?

From time to time it's probably something we all feel. There are emotions which signal that all is not well: we are lonely or sad, tired, insecure or helpless, hopeless or frustrated.

There are times to persevere and wait for a way to open up to us but also times to admit that maybe this road is going nowhere.

Sometimes we need change. And change may mean walking down a new road, visiting a new shop or getting a new job, starting a new hobby, making a new friend or even visiting a new country…

Remember it's never too late… and 'doing it' isn't 'thinking about it'… it's 'doing it'!

> **Trust God from the bottom of your heart; don't try to figure out everything on your own. Listen for God's voice in everything you do, everywhere you go; he's the one who will keep you on track.**
>
> *Proverbs 3:5-6*

Notes:

Little Thoughts from Great Cats

Chapter 22

Olly and Abi

Olly and Abi were two of a kind. They were Siamese cats who were owned by our friends. In fact maybe I should say that actually, our friends were owned by them and a visit to their home was always filled with laughter at the antics of Olly and Abi.

Highly affectionate, in fact more like dogs in behaviour and temperament, they seemed like little people wandering about at floor height. They followed our friends around wherever they were in the house and would ignore them for hours if enough attention didn't come their way.

They needed human companionship, their blue eyes imploring their desire for attention, and they would happily listen to you talk to them all day long, and often reply too. They seemed to love to meow! A lot! In fact they would let you know what they thought about everything. Their need for involvement in daily life seemed to eclipse everything (except a snooze in the sun) and they would often vocalise their requests until their demand was met.

Fun loving, full of energy and mischief, anything and everything became a prospective toy. Right pawed Abi and left pawed Olly, following the usual pattern of male and female cats, they boxed each other and anything that would move. Tissue boxes, toilet rolls, dusters or sprays were much more interesting than the traditional cat toys and their inquisitive nature and ballerina-esque bodies took them into many places to explore. Many a time from a supposed bag of shopping, a little paw would shoot out revealing it contained much more than a tin of beans!

Highly intelligent, easily bored and great explorers, they learned very fast.

"Come in," said our friends when we arrived one evening. We chose the comfy settee and then settled ourselves down. The cats looked hopeful. Was it confinement in the kitchen or an evening of joining in the fun?

"Olly, sit! Abi, sit!"

The two cats obediently sat down, all ready for a great evening to come.

We all need people.

Some individuals hate to be alone but some people use solitude and space to renew and refresh their mental and emotional state. However we are wired up, we are built for relationship.

Others teach us so much. People show us how to love and to care and how to be loved. They help us to learn to be ourselves and enhance our emotional wellbeing. They bring about change in us and help us to grow and learn about ourselves. They help us to feel included and less isolated and create security in our lives. They teach us to trust and to take risks and friends create stability.

Relationships are God given and He has placed people around you that you may grow in these things. Maybe one or two close relationships, more general friends and lots of other regular acquaintances. Some are for a season, some for longer and maybe some for a lifetime.

Who are the special people in your life?

Do you treasure and value each relationship you have for all it brings to your life?

Just as lotions and fragrance give sensual delight, a sweet friendship refreshes the soul.

Proverbs 27:9

Notes:

Chapter 23

The Orchard

Our orchard was a place of adventure. With fourteen apple trees to climb, for Porky it was a wonderland of activity. It was also a place he could escape those *cat-hating-visitors*, as he ran through their legs to the top of the garden. Or flee from the noise of any human-kitten that may come to call with its proud owner. Here he could hide, when we stood in the doorway calling his name over and over. It was only the frantic tapping of the tin opener which could bring him running.

Each tree, a different shape and height, he would edge his way along the branches as they bowed under his weight. He would jump from tree to tree doing things that seemed impossible but he would grasp the branch until he righted himself and climbed once more.

In the autumn, apples would fall as he explored these pathways in the air. Then he would find himself a secure spot where he could survey the world beneath him. He would fix his eyes on something in the grass and stare for what seemed like hours then his eyes would close as the rays of the sun bathed his fur.

At times he would stride silently through the long grass looking and listening for who knows what? There was a fence at the end of the orchard. It was one through which our weeds grew onto the neighbour's ground and every so often Mr Taylor would let us know! To Porky this was a trapeze wire as, carefully using his long tail to balance himself, he made his way along it from end to end.

Then there was his *watching* place on Boot Hill, a mound of scrap and soil where he would hide and watch the birds land in the trees chirruping as they landed, always out of reach. When butterflies came too close, he would lift his paw to play as they fluttered around his nose.

But one place was favourite above all else; nestled on my mum's lap as she read a book in the sun, knitting needles flying, eyes darting across the page, for her never a moment to waste. For Porky that was bliss. His very favourite place of all.

RELAX

Do you have a favourite place? A coffee shop? A holiday place? An armchair with a view or the place where you lived as a child? Favourite places come in all shapes and sizes. Some are far away, some next door and some even in our own home. For many people their favourite place is actually Home Sweet Home.

In our favourite place, restoration happens of mind and body. It is a place where our needs of rest, or excitement, or adventure or sleep are met. It is a place where we are able to separate ourselves from everyday worry and stress. And it is a place where we have an expectation that all these things will happen when we're there. It happened before, it will happen again and this builds up stronger links and stronger positive expectations in our mind.

A favourite place brings us pleasure, it gives us what we need.

Where are your favourite places?

> **God's a safe-house for the battered,
> a sanctuary during bad times.
> The moment you arrive, you relax;
> You're never sorry you knocked.**
>
> *Psalm 9:9-10*

Notes:

Chapter 24

The Rain

We had lots of visitors that month. Each couple would arrive early in the morning and go to the study. They would stay there for the morning, appear for lunch and return there for the afternoon.

It was a counselling opportunity for pastors and their spouses, training and also personal opportunity for prayer and counselling for each couple who pastored for Elim around our area. The study had been converted into a counselling room which left me the rest of the house free once the counsellors and the couple had begun to talk.

Right from the start of the sessions, Jock 2 loved this room. Whatever or whoever he could sense in there, he loved and he wanted to be there. Whether it was the peaceful atmosphere or the presence of the Holy Spirit, he knew it felt good.

It was a Thursday morning and Jock wasn't in the best of moods. He had tried to go out of the back door but found it was raining so had then attempted the front door in the hope that the weather was different. On discovering there was no sun in the front garden either, he stood at my feet with a pleading *please could you stop the rain* kind of meow, again and again. When I wasn't able to command the elements to his liking, he stomped off with his tail wagging (actually doing a remarkable impersonation of the dog).

When Alan and Amy arrived I showed them upstairs and they settled themselves down to begin prayer. It was towards the end of the prayer session that the previously invisible Jock 2 suddenly chose to slowly emerge from behind a plant on the top of the cupboard and jump down over the shoulder of Amy, thudding right onto the table in front of them. Amy cried out in fright and all four jumped, as startled by the creature as if it was a demon itself. Hearts beating they released Jock 2 from the room and took a break!

He slowly made his way down the stairs as I stood looking up at him. I may have been mistaken but I'm sure I saw a smug look in his eyes.

The Rain

Have you ever had a shock? Not just something that is laughed over and forgotten in an hour but a real shock?

Life is full of surprises and sometimes shocks come our way too. Shocks can debilitate us and paralyse us for a while, impeding our judgement, filling our mind so we are unable to think or operate effectively.

At times like that, routine is good. Putting the kettle on, drawing the curtains, anything which will give a sense of safety and structure. Familiar routines give us a sense of security in the middle of a foreign world. Time to talk, time to be alone helps us slowly process events and as we see friends it keeps us from isolation in our time of need.

Things take time, sometimes a long time. Time is a great healer we say, though we seldom believe it at the start of our journey of healing. But as the seasons change, so do we… maybe never the same, but eventually finding wholeness once more.

Are you tired? Worn out? Burned out on religion? Come to me. Get away with me and you'll recover your life. I'll show you how to take a real rest. Walk with me and work with me – watch how I do it. Learn the unforced rhythms of grace. I won't lay anything heavy or ill-fitting on you. Keep company with me and you'll learn to live freely and lightly.

Matthew 11:28-30

Notes:

Chapter 25

The Cat at the Bottom of our Garden

There's a cat at the bottom of our garden. She lives with six children and their mum in a house just like ours. Not that she spends much time in the house. But with six children if I were a cat, maybe I wouldn't either. Actually they are delightful children.

Lola spends most of her time sitting on the six foot fence which divides our garden from theirs. The vertical planks of wood are spaced every six inches or so, so you can see through the fence. Nevertheless, the cat likes to look *down* from the fence not *through* it. With her strong flexible body and ability to leap six times her length, she appears to be able to jump almost from floor to fence effortlessly.

Her hobby of watching our bird table is all consuming. Even with inferior daytime sight, with her wide peripheral vision, she is able to see the whole of our garden at a glance and looks engaged and stimulated for hours as she changes her position periodically in order to view it from different angles through the day.

She sees the great tits, sparrows, blue tits and robins all visit, fly away, visit and fly away and her instinctive behaviour causes her to tense at times and then relax and then tense up again as she studies their every move.

Then pigeons fly down and patter around the garden, picking up seed dropped from the table and if you stand close enough, you can hear her making a bizarre sound like chattering as in her head, she lives her dream.

She continues to watch with total fascination, heart beating I'm sure faster than its usual one hundred and twenty beats a minute! She is totally in the moment and as they fly away her eyes follow, at least for a moment, until she gazes with rapt attention once more at the bird table.

She will wait once again on the fence. At least until Jak Mac Peat, our *Yorkie-in-body-rottweiller-in-head* dog goes outside.

Then again, I know she is definitely a match for Jak!

How often do you step back and look at your life from a distance?

There are many parts to our daily life: our home, our family, our friends, our employment, our relaxation, our hobbies, our holidays, our inner world and our faith...and even more than that.

These things work together to give us a life which brings peace or brings turmoil. When our whole world seems stressed, it is often one or two parts which are in difficulty and this overflows into the whole of our experience. It's good to step back and examine our life every so often and check things are in balance.

God sees every part of the garden of our life, from the moment we are born until the moment we die. He is carefully watching from a distance but at the same time, He can be right by our side whenever we need Him.

Why not acknowledge His presence in every part of your existence today?

> **God is always on the alert, constantly on the lookout for people who are totally committed to him.**
>
> *2 Chronicles 16:9a*

Notes:

Chapter 26

Tia

Jock and Joshua Felix had just arrived home. At least Jock had, so I guessed JF had too as they never went anywhere alone. Where Jock travelled so did his brother and when JF went home so did Jock.

And then a new cat arrived on the block. With a sense of smell fourteen times greater than humans, both Jock and Joshua Felix knew that someone new was around town and maybe someone pretty interesting!

Tia moved into the flat below ours, in our *four in a block.* She was beautiful with black glossy fur and stunning green eyes. Just approaching adulthood, she carried herself with pride. She stayed out of her own home most of the time. I guess she didn't like the resident dog. In the past, Jock 2 had gone into their garden to dig up the daffodils, just to show who was in charge but not any longer! Everyone was now on their best behaviour!

And then one day Tia left home and moved in with JF and soon became his pack leader. It seemed she led the way and JF, he followed. Unfamiliar with competing for his brother's attentions, Jock was unwilling to play second fiddle so no longer did the brothers hang out together, race across the golf course or wrestle in the grass. There was a new cat in town and Tia was it. Jock would just sit in the window and watch.

And then one day Tia moved in with us. She was just there at the top of our stairs one morning when I opened the door. And the day after and the day after that too. I wanted to say *Jock, you're not playing second fiddle... get rid of her...* but soon Jock and Tia were curled up, asleep on our couch every evening. And it was JF that stared from his window.

That was until we moved house. I don't know if JF and Tia rekindled their relationship. I do know that Jock refused to leave the wardrobe for three weeks in our new house! I was just making arrangements to have Tia sent up for a visit when he appeared out of the wardrobe. And never looked back.

As cats do!

Have you ever felt envious?

Sometimes, other people get what we want! A good standard of living, a husband, a family, a nice house, a great job. And it's easy to feel that they are living the dream and we are same old, same old...

Envy does not enhance our lives. Envy is a drain on our energy, it distorts our picture, it clouds our decisions and it ends relationships.

Sometimes it seems life is unfair, and we can't control it. The truth is that often, we can't. When life seems unfair and you are powerless to change it, why not allow it to motivate you, to help you make better decisions and to urge you to higher things…?

Celebrate what you do have. Do what you can do. Turn your eyes away from them and allow them to live their life and fix your eyes ahead moving forward into your own destiny and future. And then pour your life into others who don't have the blessings that you have.

Why not begin today?

A sound mind makes for a robust body, but runaway emotions corrode the bones.

Proverbs 14:30

Notes:

Chapter 27

Cat Fight

There was a cat fight one day. The evening was still and warm in Lanzarote. Most people were out and I had left the doors open enjoying the warmth of the evening.

Suddenly breaking the stillness, came a screaming, a snarling, a sound of cats fighting. It was echoing round the apartments, magnified by the sound bouncing back and forth from wall to wall. The swimming pool below often acted as a microphone for sound and their vocal expressions were magnified many times.

I rushed out to the balcony but I could see nothing. However the noise of the fighting cats increased in volume. And then they rolled into view, a single ball of fur rolling round and round, nearer and nearer to the swimming pool nearby. I thought I recognised the grey coat of Andrew then one cat trapped the other in a corner and I could see no end to this standoff.

Andrew appeared to be holding the other cat to ransom, not allowing him to leave. I tutted from above and *the Andrew cat* looked up and turned round. I continued to tut and he fixed me with his gaze. Slowly and silently I saw the second cat move out of the corner and carefully make his way off the premises.

The grey cat continued to stare. I heard a noise by my side. It was Andrew! He had been watching from the balcony next door all the time.

He overstayed his welcome tonight. Usually five minutes at the most he stayed. Tonight, he sat looking down to the pool for thirty minutes or more. I guess, until he was sure everyone had gone.

I mean, why get your paws dirty if you don't need to?

Do you ever get involved in other people's arguments or grudges?

It's so hard, especially if we love someone, not to take on their grievances as well as our own. We can end up with very negative feelings about someone we hardly know. We can end up with situations filling our thoughts when a disagreement doesn't actually involve us. We can end up feeling stressed or depressed on behalf of another.

Effective boundaries are a good and a healthy thing to have at our disposal. Knowing what is us and what is someone else is healthy, and allowing people to learn from their own conflicts is beneficial for them.

Taking on board the angst of someone else makes us less able to think objectively and less able to help them move on. Standing aside and watching from a distance is often a good thing to do, no doubt more beneficial for everyone involved.

Are there situations you need to step out of?

Keep vigilant watch over your heart; that's where life starts.
Don't talk out of both sides of your mouth; avoid careless banter, white lies, and gossip.
Keep your eyes straight ahead; ignore all sideshow distractions.
Watch your step, and the road will stretch out smooth before you.

Proverbs 4:23-26

Notes:

Chapter 28

The Cat Lady

"**I**'ve got two new cats. Would you like to come and see them sometime?"

Invites to see new cats or dogs, kittens or puppies are never turned down by me and I gladly accepted and arranged to call in the next week or so. It took me a little longer than anticipated to get along but on a cloudy Thursday morning, I made my way to Rachel's home.

Somewhere in the back of my mind I recalled she had a few cats. No problem. I liked cats.

I pulled up outside an old bungalow at the end of a long country road. There was a black cat sitting on the doorstep. I walked up the path and knocked, bending down to scratch in between the black cat's ears. Rachel opened the door and invited me in.

I stood in the doorway for a moment, gazing round at what was before me.

"Come in, come in," she said. "I don't want Tigger and Cat Flap to get out yet. They've only been here a week."

Speechless, I looked from floor to chair to cupboard. On every available space sat or lay a cat. Black cats, white cats, tortoiseshells, Siamese and tabby cats. Cats on chairs, cats all over the settee, a cat on the TV and cats on the bookshelves. Cats in the kitchen, cats lying on the floor, cats draped over chair backs and two cats in the hearth. Every cat was different and it was amazing to think that every single one had a nose print, just like our fingerprint, which was unique.

"Sit down," she invited.

"Thank you. Where shall I sit?" I asked, as there were cats filling every available space in the room. She pushed a couple of cats off the settee and pointed to the space made for me.

"I go to cat rescue homes," she volunteered, "and I walk along by the runs. The cat chooses me to adopt them, I don't choose the cat... If one doesn't choose me, I come home without one!"

"Really?"

"They wait for a nice looking person and then purr loudly and rub up against the bars then gaze up at you with their *please take me home* eyes and you're hooked…!

"…I'm sure that's how it is with all pet adoptions," she added thoughtfully. "We don't rescue them... they sort of rescue us..."

I sat gingerly on the edge of the couch feeling, I must admit, a little overawed by the huge number of felines around me. A small ginger and white one walked along the back of the settee and pointed his bottom towards me, apparently a gesture of friendship, then a cat jumped on my knee and began kneading my lap in happiness and contentment and suddenly I was part of the family!

Taking tea and biscuits was a little difficult with, it seemed most of the cats wanting to say hello, brushing round my legs and rubbing against my arm.

Suddenly, behind me, a fight began and I turned quickly in fear almost spilling the tea. Black Eye was hissing at a large tabby.

"Oh don't worry about them," said Rachel. "Black Eye's not attacking, he's hissing in defence. He's saying *stay away*. They're always getting in each other's way. They'll settle down..." and she waved her hand at them and as she did, the tabby yawned to end the confrontation and they wandered away from each other, tails still wagging.

By now my new friend on my lap was looking at me, slowly blinking with affectionate kitty kisses of contentment. We talked a little but not a lot, as there was always someone doing something. Beauty pushing Beatrice off the cupboard. Cup Cake wanting to sit where Felix was or Tigger taking a space where old Smokey always sat. It was like having twenty six children!

That afternoon, I sat in front of my class of children thankfully. At least when I told them to line up they did (usually!) and shut up, they did (apart from a couple).

Then I began to teach and as I did, I wondered if the black cat was still on the doorstep.

Are you too busy? Do you ever feel that your life is just like that room I visited?

I've read several times just recently that busy has become the new fine. It is now apparently a modern epidemic. Some say it is a status symbol giving us a sense of importance too.

Busyness is the attempt to bridge the gap between what you have to get done and what you actually get done. But busyness causes isolation, stress, exhaustion and makes it difficult to appreciate the present moment. We are too busy thinking about what we didn't get done or what we must get done.

Many books are written about busyness and ways to organise our life in more effective ways. Listing our priorities in order, dividing the day with margins (breaks), reducing task-heavy possessions, fixing ahead a weekly day off, delegating and choosing to say "no" become a start in readdressing the chaos of our world.

Why not start to think about it today?

> **So here's what I want you to do, God helping you: Take your everyday, ordinary life – your sleeping, eating, going-to-work, and walking-around life – and place it before God as an offering.**
> **Embracing what God does for you is the best thing you can do for him.**
>
> *Romans 12:1*

Notes:

Little Thoughts from Great Cats

Chapter 29

Fergal

Helen was a cat girl. She had loved cats as long as she could remember but she'd never owned one. And so as soon as she got her own flat and settled into the city of Glasgow, she got one.

He was a long haired tabby and he was very handsome. She was certain he had an interesting heritage. He would be an indoor cat with a myriad of toys to keep him busy while she was out.

The little cat arrived from *The Cat and Dog Home* on a Saturday which Helen was pleased about as it gave her the whole weekend to settle him in. He stood in the middle of the floor looking round him in bewilderment then slowly began to wander from room to room inquisitively. Within a day he was settled and had soon found his favourite place on the windowsill looking down at the cars, people, dogs and cats passing by. There also seemed to be a particularly interesting tree outside where he could see the birds landing and taking off.

Helen named him Fergal. She didn't know why but she liked the name so Fergal, he would be.

I would guess Fergal considered Helen a very well trained pet owner. She waited on him paw and foot. She put up a pretty little tree at Christmas full of balls for him to knock off and she forgave him several little mistakes on the living room carpet. She was a little ungrateful though whenever he tried to share his fur with her when he rubbed against her legs and nestled in her lap. Even so, if he was allowed outside (which he wasn't) he would definitely catch her a mouse.

Days turned into weeks which turned into months and Fergal acquired a huge box of toys, bells, feathers and felt mice and even a life sized stuffed cat to keep him company when Helen was out. He had a scratching pole, a cat bed and a litter tray… a sort of gym, a bedroom and a bathroom, I suppose! All was well in the world of Fergal and Helen.

But Helen had this niggling thought that God was speaking to her. It wouldn't make sense to anyone else but as she filled in the forms to travel to a mission station in Malawi, she knew she was in the centre of what God wanted.

Fergal seemed even more attentive that evening when she came home, almost that he knew something was afoot.

"It wouldn't be fair for me to take him back after three years so you keep him forever," she told her friend. Then she put the phone down and cried for the rest of the evening.

The day came and Helen's friend arrived and she watched the cat bed, scratching poll, box of toys and last of all wee Fergal leave the house.

"Only you know the sacrifice I have made..." prayed Helen.

"I know the sacrifice you've made..." God's voice replied in the stillness.

"I gave up someone too."

And at that moment a ray of sunlight shone down on her and she was at peace.

Sacrifice is something difficult for us all. Giving away something precious and releasing things we love is not easy.

Sacrifice is not about what but about how. It's not the volume we give, it's the cost. It's not the amount it's the attitude.

What do we sacrifice? We can be called to sacrifice time, comfort, energy, a career, sleep, money or gifts. But when we give sacrificially, we always get more than we give because it's not what we get that brings blessings but what we give. Giving unlocks the gates to God's abundance.

When we live outside our margins, we do not have enough for ourself and we have nothing to give away. When we live within our margins then there is always enough for us and plenty to give away when the opportunity arises.

Is there a sacrifice you need to make today?

> **But he's already made it plain how to live,**
> **what to do, what God is looking for in men**
> **and women.**
> **It's quite simple: Do what is fair and just to**
> **your neighbour,**
> **be compassionate and loyal in your love,**
> **And don't take yourself too seriously –**
> **take God seriously.**
>
> *Micah 6:8*

Notes:

Chapter 30

Sleeping Cats

I read an article in the paper one day about a conservationist who takes a nine month old cheetah to bed with him and his wife. *Mummy* and *Daddy* are raising him at their home, which includes sleeping with him. He will be released one day and on that day, I imagine him wandering round the forest, frantically looking for a double bed, before nightfall!

I have never fancied taking a cheetah to bed but I do have to admit that, I guess to some people's horror, Jock 2 did sleep at the end of our bed. Many times I would wake in the night to see both Mary (the dog) and Jock flat on their backs with four feet in the air.

For some reason, I still remember the poem by Eleanor Farjeon:

> *Cats sleep anywhere,*
> *Any table, any chair,*
> *Top of piano, window ledge,*
> *In the middle, on the edge...*

And when I got a cat, I realised it was absolutely true. Jock would sleep between twelve and sixteen hours some days and twenty year old Porky, much longer. That means that by the time Jock was nine, he had only been awake for three years!

The reason there is a Jock 2, was that Jock 1, my first wonderful little ginger tomcat went out one day and sadly never came back. I remember him even now. His favourite place to sleep was on top of me. I guess there he could feel me breathing. Whenever I lay down, he would be there.

Three quarters of his sleep apparently, was snoozing when he could be alert at a moment's notice. The remaining quarter was deep sleep. Then his whiskers and paws would twitch as he dreamed and at night sometimes his snoring would wake us all! In the gloom Mary would look up in disdain at the loud sound emitting from the little animal by her side.

To me, there was no more restful a sight than to see my sleeping cat. He was a picture of peace. There was no more peaceful sound than his purring.

If you are a cat lover, stroking a cat lowers your blood pressure and releases those feel-good feelings. They are comforting and healing in difficult times with no knowledge of what they do for us.

Whenever Jock 1 came and lay on my middle, I guess he could feel my heartbeat. He would've stayed there for hours... that is, if the fridge door hadn't been opened!

Do you know inner peace right now? It's sometimes hard to find but it adds so much to our life.

It improves our happiness and makes us more productive. It increases our health and our compassion. It enhances our intelligence and strengthens our mental condition and our digestion to name just a few things. And yet we spend so little time ensuring we get to that place of peace each day.

God promises us, not just peace but a peace which passes understanding. That means when circumstances seem to dictate that peace will be nowhere to be found, it can be everywhere... over us, under us, around us, in us and totally overpowering.

Do you know God's peace today? If not then why not begin to ask Him for it now?

Don't fret or worry. Instead of worrying, pray. Let petitions and praises shape your worries into prayers, letting God know your concerns. Before you know it, a sense of God's wholeness, everything coming together for good, will come and settle you down. It's wonderful what happens when Christ displaces worry at the centre of your life.

Philippians 4:6-7

Notes:

Little Thoughts from Great Cats

Chapter 31

Mrs Harrison's Cat

I was excited at the prospect of seeing Mrs Harrison again. We turned off the main road and were soon once again in the isolation of the Shetland hillsides with voes stretching out before us and the white sand covering tiny coves as we passed by. Skuas and snipes flew through the air and the sea shimmered blue on the horizon.

We made our way past ruined buildings standing on crofts of long ago, seeing the Shetland Ponies wild on the hillsides. Stone walls stood at the side of the road and then disappeared as the roads got smaller and we could see for miles as the road wove through the hillside.

Shetland is a ruggedly beautiful group of islands which we had visited on and off since 1994. That year we had stayed in a tiny cottage right down by the sea. The only neighbour, a retired sea captain next door. Mrs Harrison's parents had owned the cottage and long gone, it gave others, like us the opportunity to experience the isolated Shetland far away from the town of Lerwick.

We made our way along the gradually narrowing roads to the west coast. Passing our beloved cottage of '94 in Sandness, we drove along the one road to Huxter until it came to an end. Here were four tiny cottages right on a cliff edge.

Mrs Harrison greeted us with a huge welcome as always and invited us into her home. Tibbles the tabby cat lay on the chair and she pushed him off so we could sit down. He moved under the bench to where there was a bone and began to lick it using the backward spikes on his tongue to break off and grip the meat. I remembered Jock's tongue felt like sandpaper.

"He likes bones," Mrs Harrison informed us, as though cats and bones were the most natural thing in the world.

As she made the tea and brought out scones, I looked around. I could hear the seagulls outside and the wind blowing around the cottage and all I could see through the window was the sea below. This was all Tibbles had known. Rocks down which to climb, seagulls to watch and fish to catch. Grass to snooze in and nightfall to explore and hunt reptiles, mice, birds and who knows what else? Back paws following the track of his front paws to limit his tracks and noise, he would be a silent moonlight hunter. No light pollution here!

I thought of Jock back at home in the City of Glasgow. So far removed from here. Yet was he happy? He seemed so. They often say that cats are more attached to the place than the people. That they will return to an old house or even happily remain there with new owners.

Tibbles slowly got up and made his way out of the room.

"He won't go far," said Mrs Harrison. "Not nowadays..."

I looked outside and thought of the thousands of cats on the island, and in the UK, all bringing that something special to the lives of their owners. I'm glad that God made cats...

Have you ever known a cat? If so, what did he teach you?

Life is somewhat like an island, there are beautiful parts, and there are parts which have been dangerous. There are days when the sky is blue and seasons when the wind howls and the storms rage. There are old ruins in places and new life in others as the spring flowers emerge. There are parts which are busy, full of people and sometimes times of isolation and loneliness.

Cats teach us many things. They teach us to never give up, to enjoy every day and to live in the moment. They teach us to never lose our curiosity, to love unconditionally and to rest and relax regularly. They teach us appreciation, not to worry and give us things to laugh at. They never judge and they never fail.

It's many years since I owned Jock 2 but writing this book has again highlighted the wonder of this, one of God's creatures.

Am I tempted..? Maybe???

I came so they can have real and eternal life, more and better life than they ever dreamed of.

John 10:10

Notes:

And just in case you're *not* fed up with cat stories...

Epilogue

I was just finishing this book, reading through each chapter and making corrections when this last story took place:

We were just arriving for a week's break in Lanzarote, our favourite holiday destination, and as we ascended the several flights of stairs to the apartment, Kevin noticed a little cat under the stairway as we passed. We went back to look and saw that with her, she had three small kittens. This was one of the many street cats, but only young herself, she had made her way into the complex and found a shaded place under a stairway to have her kittens.

A few days later we saw the kittens left alone. Presumably hungry, she had gone off to hunt for food. But the next day, others must have noticed as someone had kindly put down a bowl with water and some cat biscuits and an old blanket for the kittens to snuggle into.

I could not resist glancing each time we passed by and as the week went on I saw more food arriving each day...on one morning two freshly cooked, large kippers! There was tinned cat food and dry cat biscuits and fresh water every day as all the cat lovers of the complex made an effort to see she was well fed and didn't need to stray very far.

Nevertheless, having kittens is a dangerous occupation for a street cat. Other cats could easily get over the fence into the complex and attack the kittens and the complex caretaker was not happy at having a street cat breeding in his empire. Also, where she was situated was a main thoroughfare for many residents, not the quiet, secluded usual choice for a new mother and her kittens.

One morning I came down the stairs and met the little mother cat on the stairway above hers. As I approached she growled at me, definitely in attack mode and ran down the stairs to her beloved offspring. I quietly followed her and saw only two kittens. My heart sank. My fear was that kitten number three had somehow escaped from the family and disappeared. I stood looking at them in dismay. He certainly wasn't there any longer.

Just then I heard a high pitched meowing coming from upstairs. As I searched, there was the third tiny musketeer! Two kittens on the floor below and one above! No idea how he had got there but with the help of someone, the little runaway was carefully moved back into his nest.

We went out for the day and passed by her nest on our way back in. Mum and kittens all gone! On ascending the stairs we found the whole family in the new place I had seen her that morning. A flitting had taken place. She was obviously determined to move house that morning and was in the process when we had moved her back again! But this was an even busier place with no shelter from the blazing sun. Nevertheless as *mother knows best*, we left her there. Before long a little box, for shade, two little bowls of food and water had appeared and now she was set up in her new home.

But the kittens were getting bigger and starting to move about, inquisitive as to what was around them. They were certainly in danger from predators and also from the hot sun.

The next day I walked past and they were gone. I asked the complex manager as he passed.

"Yes, they've gone to Yaiza," he assured me, obviously relieved himself. "They will be fostered until they're old enough to leave mum then she and the kittens will all go off to their own forever homes."

I stood for a moment and imagined the kittens, safe and cared for. Lying in the sun, fishing down by the water, growing into strong, healthy, well fed cats. Having kittens of their own, joining the huge family of cats in the sun.

I love happy endings!

It's good to know that you and I can have a forever home. That when this life is done, the Bible says that we have a forever home in heaven.

God made heaven and earth, and heaven is His home. He sent Jesus down to earth to tell us the truth and to provide a way for us to enter heaven. When He died and was resurrected, He went back to God in heaven.

Heaven is a place where there is no death, no mourning, crying or pain.

It is a place of peace where we can live forever.

Jesus is getting your place ready for you for the day you leave this earth. Until that day, He promises to be with you here on earth, to guide you, direct you and guard your life. And His home in heaven is available to anyone who believes and trusts what He says.

It's planned for you. It's your forever home.

Don't let this throw you. You trust God, don't you? Trust me. There is plenty of room for you in my Father's home.

John 14:1-2a

Notes:

Little Thoughts from Great Cats

If you have never begun your own relationship with Jesus, why not do that today by praying the prayer below:

Thank you God that you are preparing a forever home for all who believe in you.

I want to say before you today that I believe in you.

I am sorry for the wrong things that I think, I say and I do.

Thank you that you died for my sin and you forgive me.

I ask you to fill me with your love and be with me every day until I meet you one day, in my forever home in heaven.

I look forward to my new life with you by my side.

In Jesus' Name I pray.

Amen

But ask the animals what they think –
let them teach you;
let the birds tell you what's going on.
Put your ear to the earth – learn the basics.
Listen – the fish in the ocean will tell you
their stories.
Isn't it clear that they all know and agree,
that God is sovereign, that he holds all things
in his hand.

Job 12:7-10a

Other books by Margaret Peat

The White Elephant

Eleven real life stories about people who dealt with issues such as loss, inferiority, and forgiveness. A devotional book to work through your own issues as you read.

The Seagull

Eleven more stories about real people dealing with life topics such as putting God in a box, the power of words, the effect of sowing and reaping. A devotional book for you.

Dear Sally

Presented in the form of letters which Margaret sent to a close friend, this book works through eleven powerful life principles to weave into your own life and experience.

Great Thoughts from a Little Dog

If you don't like dogs, don't buy this book! A 31 day devotional for dog lovers based on the benefits of knowing God as Father. Enjoy a dog parable a day!

Across the Brook

Kevin and Margaret share their individual stories as they journeyed along their first 25 years of life. This book shows how anyone can discover a perfect Father's love.

The Journey

A spiritual journey into God's presence borne out of messages Margaret has ministered over the years. It is packed with wisdom, insight, and a good dose of humour!

Family at War

Life was tough for Giovanni as he arrived in the UK in 1869. Based around the First World War years, we read of the battles he faces for his family and himself. We still face very similar battles today and this book gives practical and deep spiritual insight to build up, encourage and inspire those who belong to God's family at war.

The Well

Do you have a date with destiny? You will never read the story of the Samaritan woman who met Jesus at the well in the same light again. Margaret brings this story to life and makes the woman, one of the most well known in the New Testament, a real character with a history before that life changing meeting.

For orders please contact: KMPeat@aol.com